SEVENTH-DAY ADVENTIST CHURCH <u>QUICK OVERVIEW</u>

60 KEY QUESTIONS ANSWERED IN UNDER 60 MINUTES

Philip de Rivaz, M.A.

All rights reserved. No portion of this book may be reproduced, stored in a retrieval system, or transmitted in any form or by any means – electronic, mechanical, photocopy, recording, scanning, or other – except for brief quotations in critical reviews or articles, without the prior written permission of the author.

Published from the UK, © 2024.

For more information or for enquiries about bulk orders, please e-mail info@philipderivaz.co.uk or visit www.philipderivaz.co.uk.

ISBN: 9798335475259

Dedicated to my dearest Kate and her family – Luke 18:27.

Introduction

Coming from a different Christian background, I have researched the Adventist Church in great detail (currently doing a PhD). From the viewpoint of an outsider trying to make sense of the church, here is a quick overview for others in a similar boat, or even current members wanting to learn more.

With 60 relevant pages of facts about the church, each can be read in under 1 minute, giving a total reading time of under 60 minutes. There are six categories, with 10 pages per category: Who? What? Why? When? Where? and How? Ellen White, as the key person in the Adventist Church, is quoted on each page.

However, the key point is that this is just a brief overview, as a precursor to a potential lifetime of learning. There is far more to study than is in this short book and this serves merely to act as a "first page of learning".

Philip de Rivaz, 8th August, 2024

Author Profile

Philip de Rivaz is a UK theologian, who holds a Postgraduate Diploma and also an MA in theology from Newbold College and is presently studying a full-time theology PhD from Anglia Ruskin University. In addition, he holds a Major in English literature, with a Minor in creative writing degree from UEA.

He is the co-editor of "Newbold Church Testimonials 3", is currently writing a longer book, developing an Adventist course and makes videos: www.PhilipdeRivaz.co.uk.

Index – 1

Who?

1. Who was Ellen White?
2. Who are the "remnant"?
3. Who was James White?
4. Who was Joseph Bates?
5. Who was William Miller?
6. Who was Hiram Edson?
7. Who was "Willie" White?
8. Who was Edson White?
9. Who was John Harvey Kellogg?
10. Who is Ted Wilson?

What?

11. What is the Great Controversy?
12. What was the Millerite Movement?
13. What was the Great Disappointment?
14. What is the Spirit of Prophecy?
15. What are the "Conflict of the Ages" books?
16. What does "Seventh-day Adventist" mean?
17. What is the Heavenly Sanctuary?
18. What is the "health message"?
19. What are the Three Angels' Messages?
20. What is the Millennium?

Index – 2

Why?

21. Why was Ellen White crucial?
22. Why did Ellen White write so much?
23. Why should you become an Adventist?
24. Why do Adventists live longer?
25. Why are many Adventists vegetarian/vegan?
26. Why is the Adventist Church structured as it is?
27. Why do Adventists tithe?
28. Why is there sin in the world?
29. Why will the lost be annihilated?
30. Why has Jesus not returned?

When?

31. When did Jesus first exist?
32. When was the world created?
33. When is the Sabbath?
34. When was the Adventist Church formed?
35. When was the first Adventist foreign missionary?
36. When was "righteousness by faith" debated?
37. When will we understand Bible prophecies?
38. When will the "end times" be?
39. When will there be a "time of "great trouble"?
40. When will Jesus return?

Index – 3

Where?

41. Where is Jesus now?
42. Where do Adventists get their doctrines from?
43. Where are Adventist churches located?
44. Where can one read Adventist books?
45. Where are Adventist schools and universities?
46. Where is the Adventist headquarters?
47. Where is the Adventist Church growing fastest?
48. Where does ADRA (humanitarian agency) operate?
49. Where do people go when they die?
50. Where is the New Jerusalem?

How?

51. How difficult were the lives of early Adventists?
52. How often did Ellen White speak publicly?
53. How many books has Ellen White written?
54. How is Ellen White criticised?
55. How can I become an Adventist?
56. How are Adventists saved?
57. How fast is the Adventist Church growing?
58. How will the world end?
59. How will things be on the New Earth?
60. How often should we read Ellen White's writings?

Abbreviations for Ellen White Books

1SM – Selected Messages, Book 1
3SM – Selected Messages, Book 3
1T – Testimonies for the Church, Vol. 1
3T – Testimonies for the Church, Vol. 3
4T – Testimonies for the Church, Vol. 4
5T – Testimonies for the Church, Vol. 5
9T – Testimonies for the Church, Vol. 9
AA – Acts of the Apostles
AH – Adventist Home
AY – An Appeal to the Youth
Broadside – Broadside 3 April 7, 1847, par. 2
CCh – Counsels for the Church
CD – Counsels on Diet and Foods
CET – Christian Experience & Teachings of Ellen White
CH – Counsels on Health
ChL – Christian Leadership
CIHS – Christ In His Sanctuary
CM – Colporteur Ministry
CME – A Call to Medical Evangelism
DA – The Desire of Ages
DD – Darkness Before Dawn
DG – Daughters of God
Ed – Education
Ev – Evangelism
EW – Early Writings
FW – Faith and Works
GC – The Great Controversy

GRC – God's Remnant Church
GrH – The Great Hope
Hvn – Heaven
LDE – Last Day Events
LS – Life Sketches of Ellen White
Mar – Maranatha
MTC – Ministry to the Cities

Abbreviations for Bible Books

1 Thess. – 1 Thessalonians
Eph. – Ephesians
Ex. – Exodus
Jer. – Jeremiah
Lev. – Leviticus
Matt. – Matthew
Rev. – Revelation
Rom. – Romans

Other

28 Fundamental Beliefs – www.adventist.org/beliefs
Ellen White Writings – www.egwwritings.org

1. Who was Ellen White?

Ellen White (née Harmon; 1827–1915) was one of the key founders of the Seventh-day Adventist Church. In her childhood she suffered a serious facial injury. After overcoming this setback, she went on to help establish and then guide the Adventist Church through her visions from God, thereby guiding people back to the Bible.

"Little heed is given to the Bible, and the Lord has given a lesser light to lead men and women to the greater light." *(CM, p. 102)*

2. **Who** are the "remnant"?

Whilst "the remnant" (*Rev. 12:17*) can be considered as those faithful from any church, in the "end times" it refers to the belief that the Adventist Church has a key role to play in keeping the commandments and preaching Jesus' soon return.

"The message of Christ's righteousness is to sound from one end of the earth to the other to prepare the way of the Lord." (*LDE, p. 137*)

3. Who was James White?

James White (1821–1881) was a successful preacher from a Christian organisation called the "Christian Connexion". Like Ellen White, he had overcome a health problem from his youth (vision). He married her in 1846 and went on to initiate the publishing work, write books and speak publicly, driving the Adventist Church forward. After recovering multiple times from declining health, he finally died through overwork, having achieved much.

"The hand of God in his restoration was most apparent. Probably no other one upon whom such a blow has fallen ever recovered." (*1T, p. 574*)

4. Who was Joseph Bates?

Joseph Bates (1792–1872), along with Ellen and James White was a co-founder of the Adventist Church. He had originally been a sea captain and after a vision from Ellen White about planets that he felt could have only been revealed by God (from his work he had studied about the planets for years), he became a believer in her prophetic gift. Additionally, he introduced the Whites to the Sabbath truth.

"He had early embraced the Advent faith, and was an active laborer in the cause." (*LS, p. 84*)

5. Who was William Miller?

William Miller (1782–1849) led the "Advent Movement" that preceded the Adventist Church. After his faith had lapsed, he had a religious conversion, following miraculously surviving fighting in a battle against Britain. From much Bible study, he believed that Jesus was returning in 1843. His evangelistic work spread through the United States and the rest of the world during his lifetime.

"Miller found the literal, personal coming of Christ to be plainly taught in the Scriptures." (*GC, p. 275*)

6. Who was Hiram Edson?

Following the Great Disappointment of 1844 when Jesus had not returned as expected (see Appendix 1), Hiram Edson (1806–1882) had a revelation when walking across a field: Jesus had gone to the Most Holy Place of the Heavenly Sanctuary. This change of doctrine was fundamental to the future Adventist Church's direction.

"He, for the first time, entered on that day into the second apartment of that sanctuary," (*CIHS, p. viii*)

7. Who was "Willie" White?

Ellen White gave birth to four sons, two of whom survived beyond her lifetime. The youngest surviving was "Willie" White, who was a faithful assistant to his mother and went on to undertake high-level Adventist leadership roles.

"Now, dear Willie, try to do right always, and then no black mark will be set down against you; and when Jesus comes he will call for that good boy Willie White," (*AY, p. 22*)

8. Who was Edson White?

James Edson White was the second son of Ellen White. Whilst he originally had been involved in the Adventist mission he drifted away, before returning and doing much work.

"Edson, my dear boy, give yourself to God. Wherein you have erred, frankly acknowledge it by confession and humility." (*DG, p. 250*)

9. Who was John Harvey Kellogg?

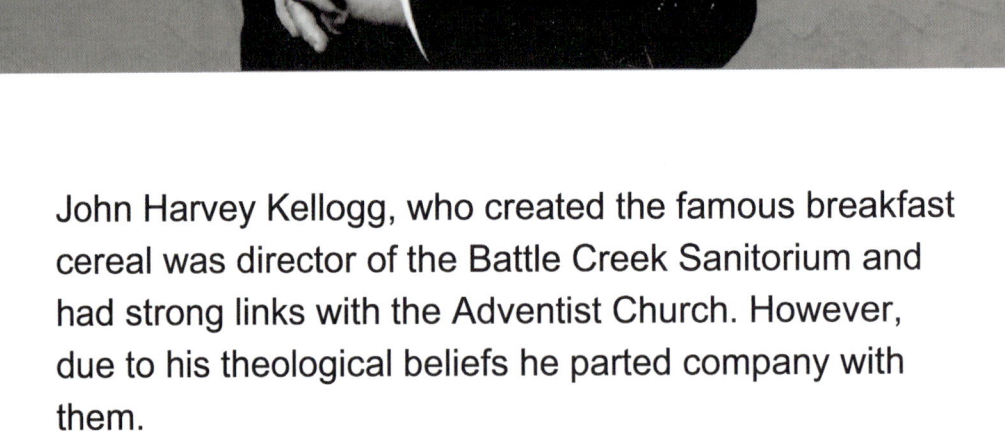

John Harvey Kellogg, who created the famous breakfast cereal was director of the Battle Creek Sanitorium and had strong links with the Adventist Church. However, due to his theological beliefs he parted company with them.

"Dr. Kellogg had taken up the medical missionary work, I encouraged him with heart and soul," (CH, p. 562)

10. Who is Ted Wilson?

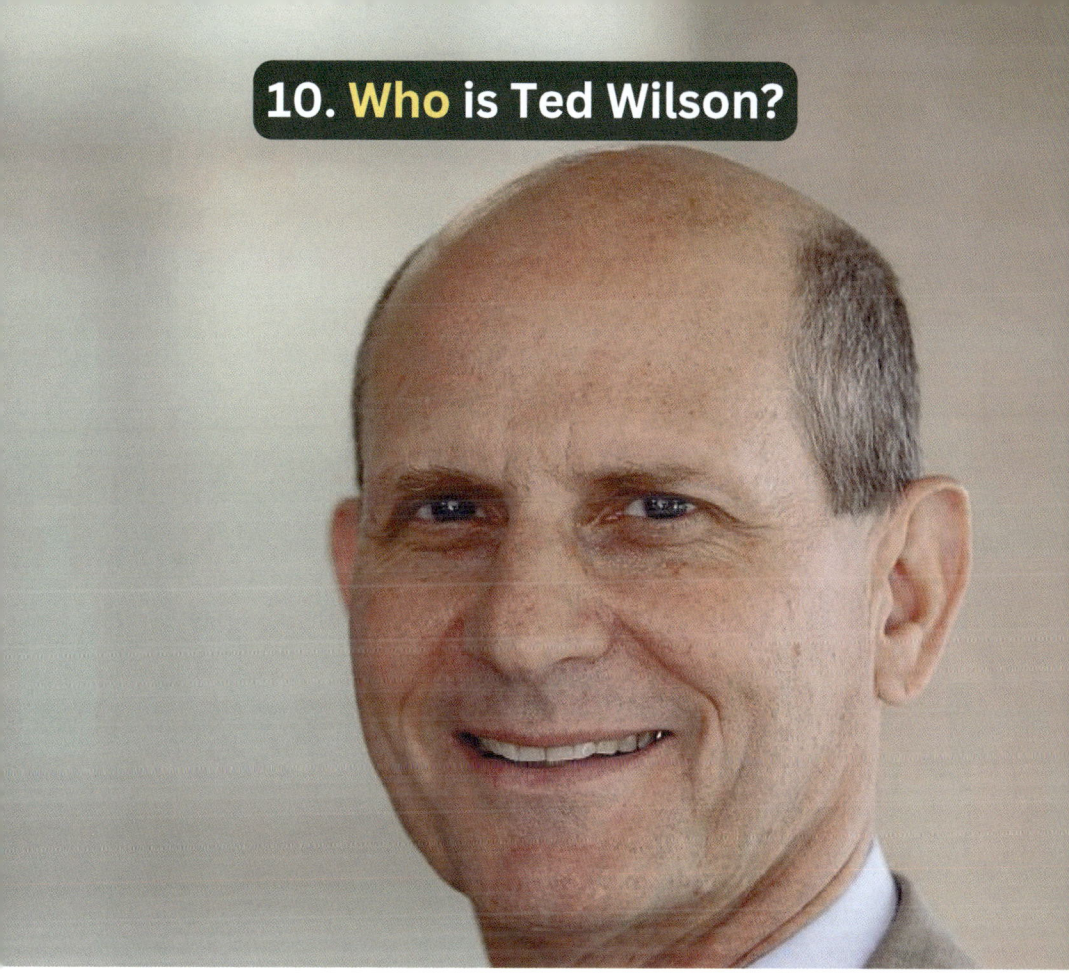

Ted Wilson is the current global president of the Seventh-day Adventist Church, as of mid-2024. He is the son of Neal Wilson and both presidents have seen steady church growth during their tenures.

"The Lord calls for wise men to preside over His work and to be faithful shepherds of His flock." (*ChL, p. 31*)

11. **What** is the Great Controversy?

A key motif within the writings of Ellen White is the cosmic "great controversy" between good and evil, after "war in heaven" (*Rev. 12:17*). One of her most famous books is titled *The Great Controversy*.

"But to every one of us comes at times a longing to know more of the great controversy. How did the controversy begin? Or was it always here?" (*GC, p. 3*)

12. What was the Millerite Movement?

The Millerite Movement began in 1831, driven by William Miller a Baptist preacher, proclaiming the soon return of Jesus.

"At the age of thirteen I heard William Miller deliver his second course of lectures in Portland, Maine... And when the invitation was given for church members and sinners to come forward for prayers, I embraced the first opportunity," (*EW, p. 12*)

13. What was the Great Disappointment?

The Millerite movement expected Jesus to return in 1844, having mistakenly interpreted the Bible to predict His return to earth on 22nd October that year (see a prophetic chart initially calculating 1843, above and the full chart in Appendix 2). Needless to say, the Christians who believed this experienced great disappointment.

> "In the great disappointment their faith was tested as was that of the Hebrews at the Red Sea." (*GC, p. 389*)

14. What is the Spirit of Prophecy?

The "spirit of prophecy" (*Rev. 19:10*) refers to the belief that God's remnant church possesses gifts from God, including the prophetic ministry, as demonstrated through the life of Ellen White.

"The remnant of the gospel church will have the gifts. War will be waged against them because they keep the commandments of God and have the testimony of Jesus Christ. (Revelation 12:17.) In Revelation 19:10, the testimony of Jesus is defined to be the spirit of prophecy." (*EW, p. 148*)

15. What are the "Conflict of the Ages" books?

The "Conflict of the Ages" series by Ellen White comprises five books, tracing events from the Garden of Eden to the New Jerusalem: *Patriarchs and Prophets*, *Prophets and Kings*, *The Desire of Ages*, *Acts of the Apostles* and *The Great Controversy*.

"By the plan of redemption, however, a way has been opened whereby the inhabitants of the earth may still have connection with heaven." (*GC, p. v*)

16. What does "Seventh-day Adventist" mean?

The name "Seventh-day Adventist" was chosen on October 1, 1860, in Battle Creek, Michigan, USA, to represent Jesus' soon return and the seventh day Sabbath.

"The Lord has made us the depositaries of His law; He has committed to us sacred and eternal truth, which is to be given to others in faithful warnings, reproofs, and encouragement." (*5T, p. 347*)

17. What is the Heavenly Sanctuary?

The mobile "Sanctuary" (*Ex. 15:17*) that the Israelites used and set up to worship God was a reflection of an actual Heavenly Sanctuary, where Jesus is now ministering.

"He carried the minds of his hearers beyond the earthly service and the ministry of Christ in the heavenly sanctuary, to the time when, having completed His mediatorial work, Christ would come again in power and great glory, and establish His kingdom on the earth." (*AA, p. 156*)

18. What is the "health message"?

Ellen White supported the spread of the "health message", which can be encapsulated by the acronym "N.E.W.S.T.A.R.T.". This stands for Nutrition, Exercise, Water, Sunlight, Temperance, Air, Rest and Trust in God.

> "Health and temperance work has always been a part of world evangelism. Many important reforms in healthful living are recognized as being closely interwoven with the Advent gospel message." (*CME, p. 6*)

19. What are the Three Angels' Messages?

The Three Angels' Messages (*Rev. 14:6-11*) are the final "alarm" given, warning the earth to follow God and avoid false worship.

"The three angels of Revelation 14 represent the people who accept the light of God's messages and go forth as His agents to sound the warning throughout the length and breadth of the earth." (*CCh, p. 58*)

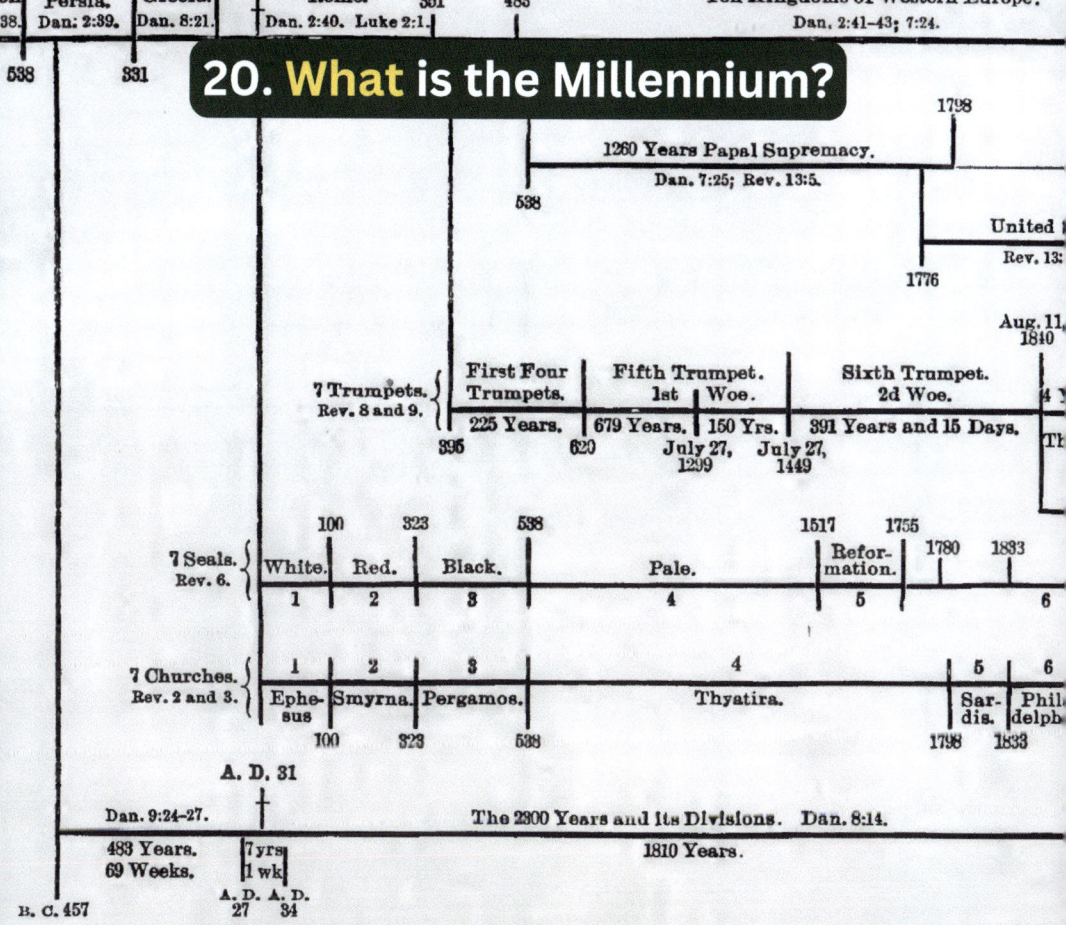

20. What is the Millennium?

The Millennium is the doctrine that Jesus, along with the resurrected and living saved, will go to Heaven for "a thousand years" (*Rev. 20:2*), to review everyone's life cases. Meanwhile, Satan and his angels will be imprisoned on the desolate earth.

"At the close of the 1000 years, Christ returns to the earth accompanied by the redeemed and a retinue of angels. He bids the wicked dead arise to receive their doom." (*GrH, p. 82*)

21. Why was Ellen White crucial?

Many other splinter groups arose after the Great Disappointment of 1844, the majority of which faded into obscurity, or achieved less success. Through Ellen White's extensive guidance, the church has continued to thrive.

"...when a voice said to me, "Look again, and look a little higher." At this I raised my eyes, and saw a straight and narrow path, cast up high above the world. On this path the Adventist people were traveling to the city". (*EW, p. 32*)

22. **Why** did Ellen White write so much?

Ellen White received many revelations from God to instruct the Adventist church and as the most translated female author in history went on to write about a diverse range of topics.

> "I saw an angel swiftly flying to me. He quickly carried me from the earth to the Holy City. In the city I saw a temple, which I entered. I passed through a door before I came to the first veil. This veil was raised, and I passed into the Holy Place." (*Broadside 3 April 7, 1847, par. 2*)

23. Why should you become an Adventist?

There are many reasons to become an Adventist, such as the health message, profound truths and spiritual insight. They also have supportive churches and interesting sermons.

"The truths were so clear, so grand, so vital, that it was difficult to sense that upon them rested the responsibility of imparting this light to others." (*CIHS, p. x*)

24. Why do Adventists live longer?

Adventists tend to live longer due to a healthy lifestyle, which includes not smoking or drinking and a nourishing plant-based diet. The Adventist Church in Loma Linda, USA, is now identified as one of the five global "blue zones".

> "We are under solemn obligations to God to keep the spirit pure and the body healthy, that we may be a benefit to humanity and render to God perfect service." (*AH, p. 93*)

25. Why are many Adventists vegetarian/vegan?

Ellen White had previously been a prolific meat eater and in very poor health. Guided to follow a plant-based diet, her health improved and she lived to old age, encouraging others to follow suit.

"Great care should be taken when the change is made from a flesh meat to a vegetarian diet to supply the table with wisely prepared, well-cooked articles of food." (*CD, p. 89*)

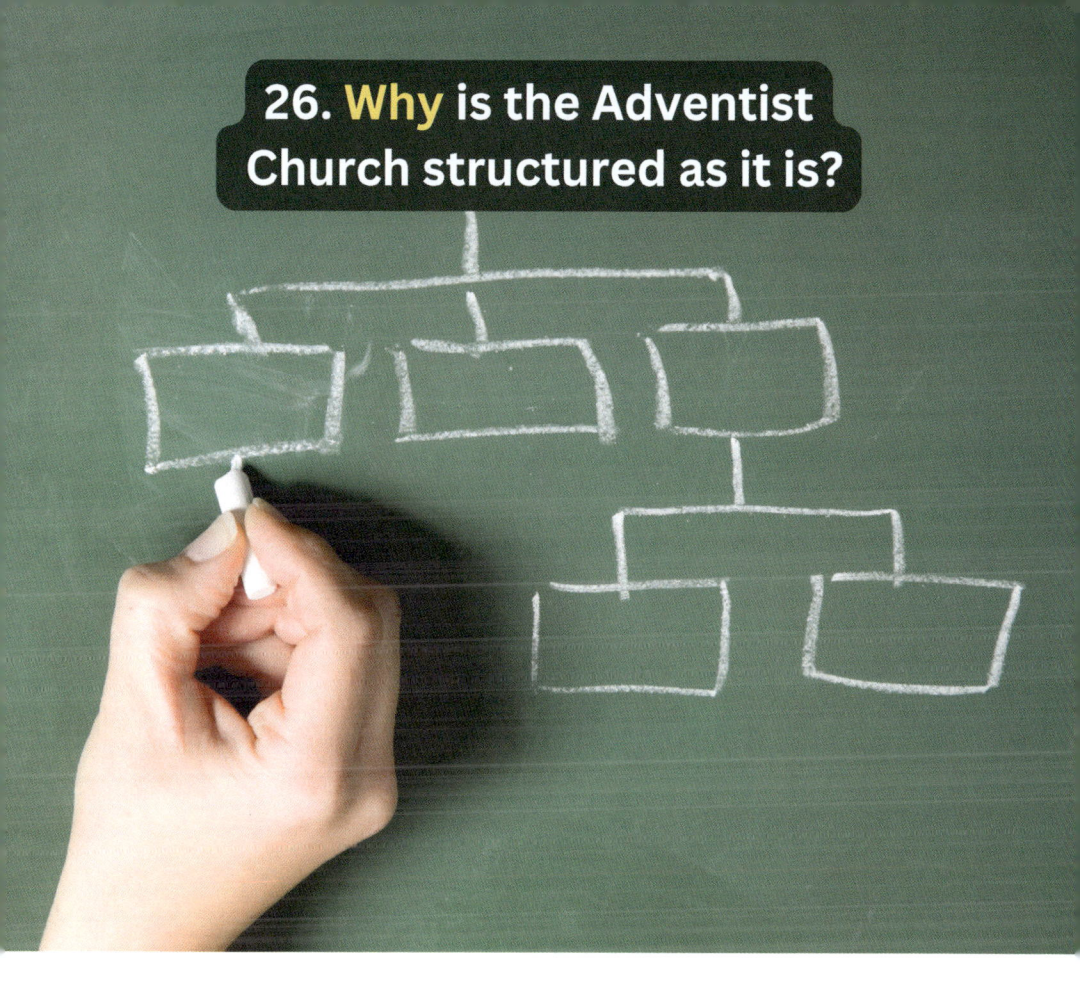

26. Why is the Adventist Church structured as it is?

To represent and be accountable, the Adventist Church is structured with local churches, local Conferences / Missions, Union Conferences / Missions, and the General Conference with its 13 divisions.

"The church is God's appointed agency for the salvation of men. It was organized for service, and its mission is to carry the gospel to the world." (*AA, p. vii*)

27. Why do Adventists tithe?

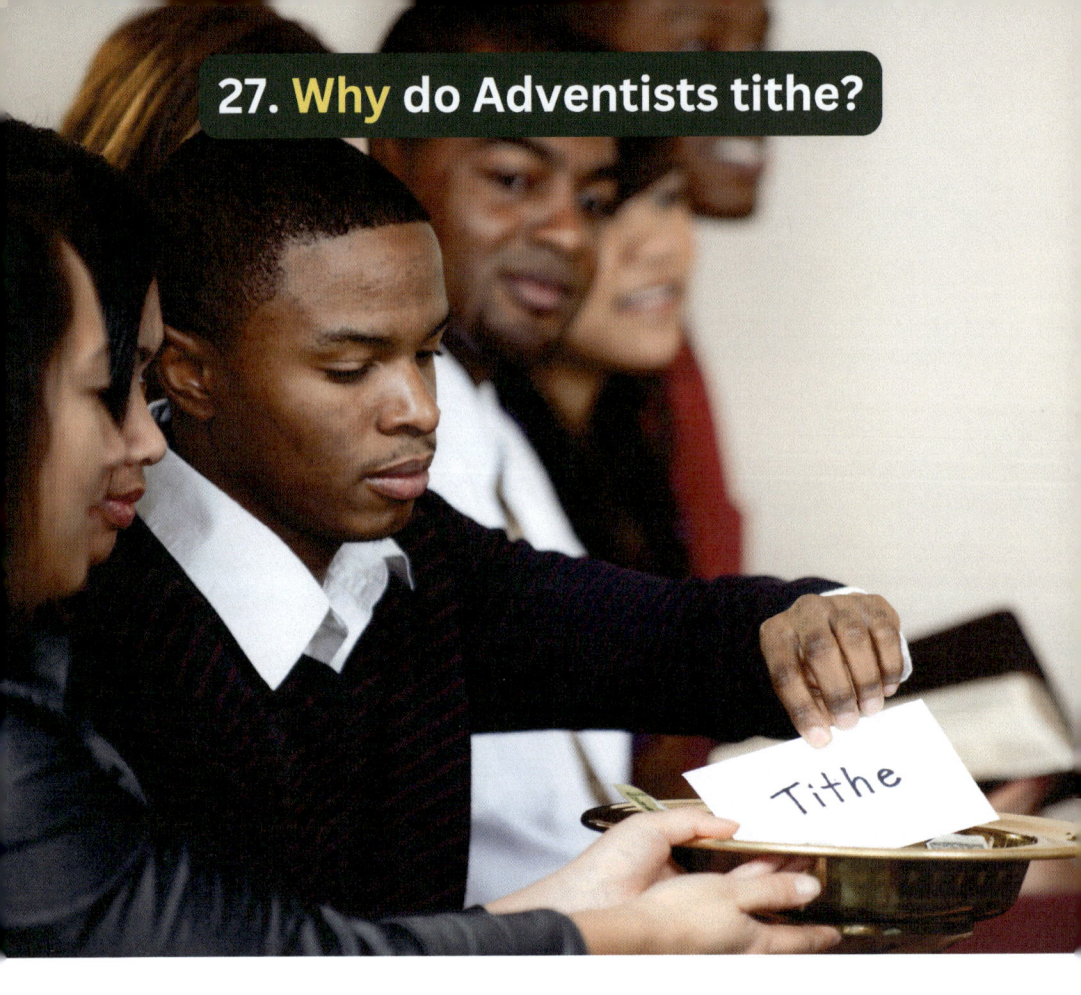

Tithing, which was originally mentioned in the Old Testament (*Lev. 27:32*), is utilised to finance church operations.

"God has made the proclamation of the gospel dependent upon the labors and the gifts of His people. Voluntary offerings and the tithe constitute the revenue of the Lord's work." (*AA, p. 49*)

28. Why is there sin in the world?

Adventists hold to the Biblical belief, that God had instructed Adam and Eve not to eat from the "tree of knowledge". After being tricked by the devil to do so, "sin entered into the world" (*Rom. 5:12*).

"Eve had been the first in transgression; and she had fallen into temptation by separating from her companion, contrary to the divine direction. It was by her solicitation that Adam sinned, and she was now placed in subjection to her husband." (*AH, p. 87*)

29. Why will the lost be annihilated?

The sinful lost would not be happy in Heaven. However, being tormented for eternity, as other churches teach, also appears unreasonable. Therefore, God who 'is able to destroy' (*Matt. 10:28*), will sadly destroy the unsaved.

"The sinner could not be happy in God's presence; he would shrink from the companionship of holy beings. Could he be permitted to enter heaven, it would have no joy for him." (*Hvn, p. 65*)

30. Why has Jesus not returned?

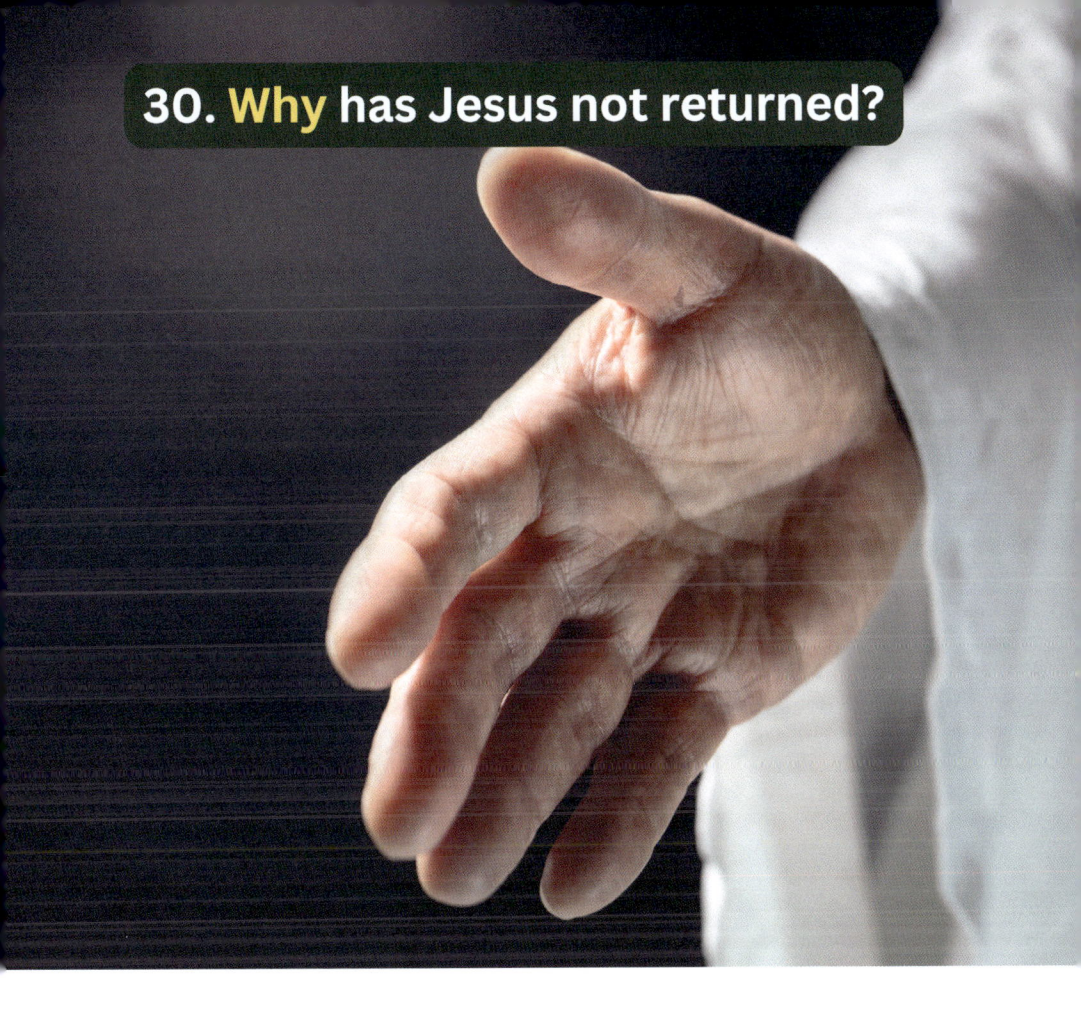

God is waiting for people to be properly prepared and for the final warning of the Three Angels' Messages, for receiving "eternal life" (*John 10:28*), to be spread around the world.

"Had the church of Christ done her appointed work as the Lord ordained, the whole world would before this have been warned, and the Lord Jesus would have come to our earth in power and great glory." (*DA, p. 553*)

31. When did Jesus first exist?

Adventists hold to the standard Christian belief that Jesus, "the Word", co-existed eternally with God, from "the beginning" (*John 1:1*).

"Christ is the pre-existent, self-existent Son of God.... In speaking of his pre-existence, Christ carries the mind back through dateless ages. He assures us that there never was a time when He was not in close fellowship with the eternal God." (*Ev, p. 557*)

32. When was the world created?

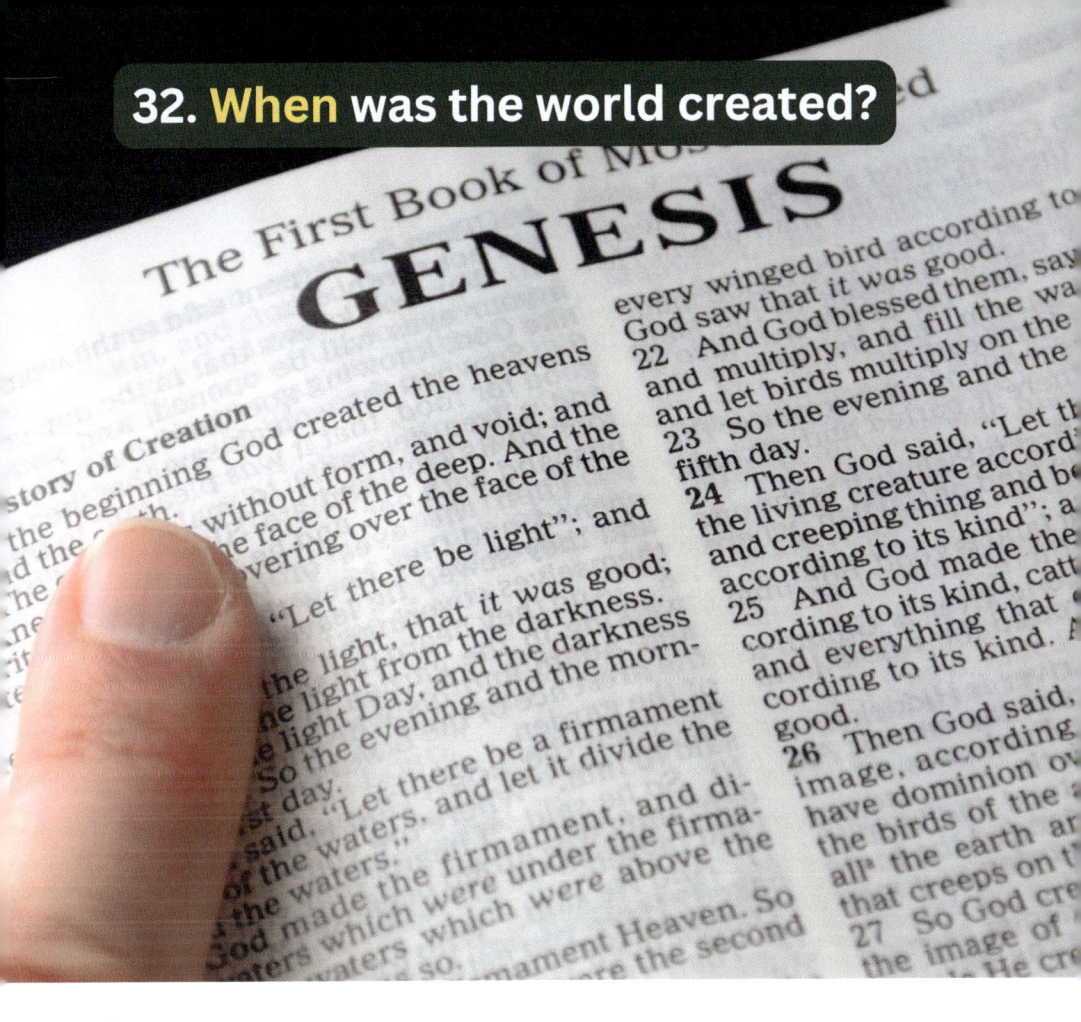

The Adventist Church teaches the Biblical Genesis doctrine that Adam and Eve were created, rather than having evolved.

> "God created man in His own image. Here is no mystery. There is no ground for the supposition that man was evolved by slow degrees of development from the lower forms of animal or vegetable life." (DG, p. 16)

33. When is the Sabbath?

The Bible Sabbath is the seventh day of the week, as per the fourth of the Ten Commandments (*Ex. 20:8*). Specifically, it is from sunset on Friday to sunset on Saturday each week.

"God rested on the seventh day, and set it apart for man to observe in honor of His creation of the heavens and the earth in six literal days. He blessed and sanctified and made holy the day of rest." (*3SM, p. 284*)

34. When was the Adventist Church formed?

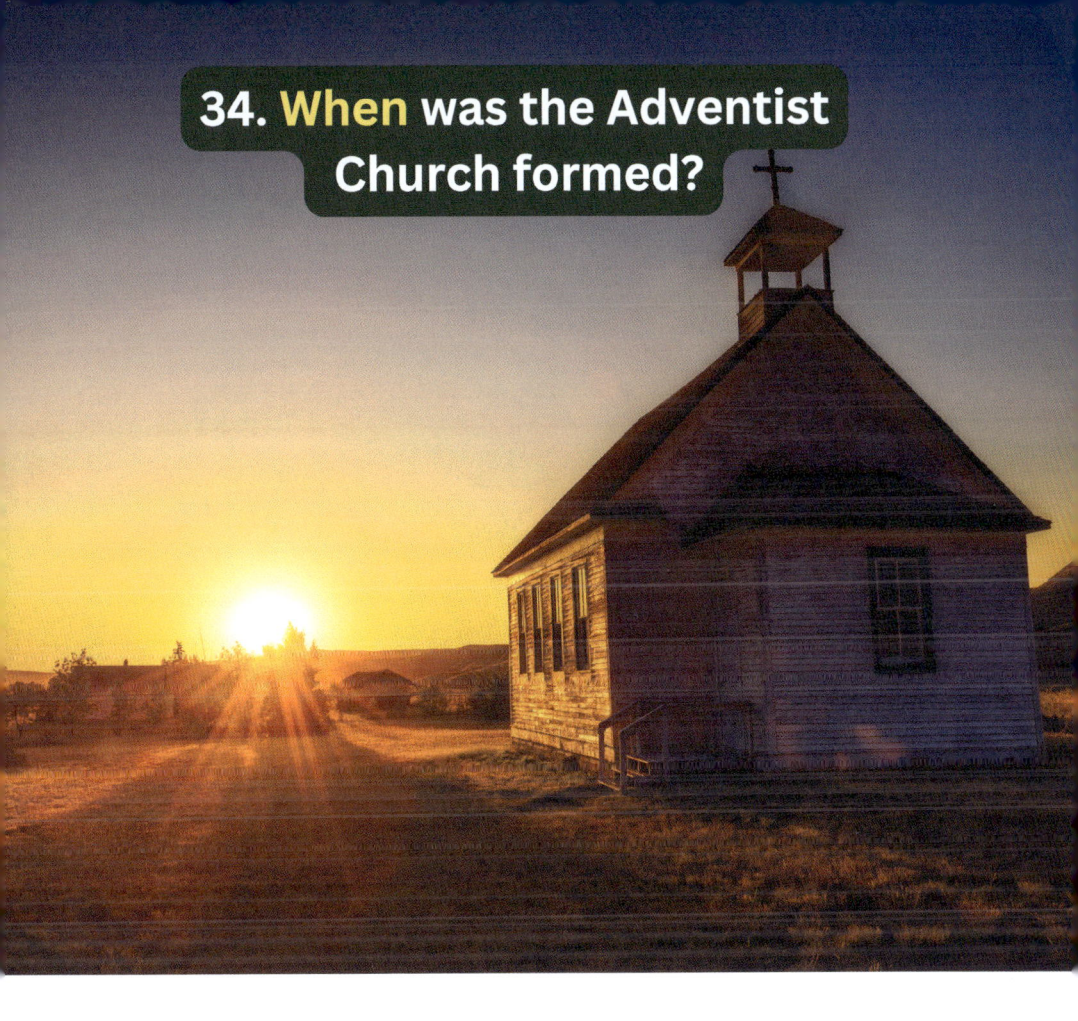

The Seventh-day Adventist Church was officially founded on May 21, 1863, Battle Creek, Michigan, in the United States.

"God has a church on earth who are lifting up the downtrodden law, and presenting to the world the Lamb of God that taketh away the sins of the world." (*GRC p. 40*)

35. When was the first Adventist foreign missionary?

J.N. Andrews was the first official overseas missionary; he went to Europe in 1874 as per Ellen White's missionary imperative.

> "The gospel commission is the great missionary charter of Christ's kingdom. The disciples were to work earnestly for souls, giving to all the invitation of mercy." (*AA, p. 18*)

36. When was "righteousness by faith" debated?

The issue of being "justified by faith" (*Rom. 5:1*) was especially contested in the 1888 conference in Minneapolis, where there were disputing camps, with Ellen White supporting the Biblical view.

"Separate humanity from divinity, and you can try to work out your own righteousness from now till Christ comes, and it will be nothing but a failure." (*FW, p. 55*)

37. When will we understand Bible prophecies?

Through Ellen White and others, Adventists have extensive understanding of Bible prophecy. She has written about the subject, such as in the book *The Great Controversy*.

> "Thus far every specification of the prophecies is strikingly fulfilled, and the beginning of the seventy weeks is fixed beyond question at 457 B.C., and their expiration in A.D. 34." (*CIHS, p. 56*)

38. When will the "end times" be?

Some Adventists believe that we are already in the "end times". Whilst Jesus is returning soon (see Appendix 3), things are due to get far worse, such as not being able to "buy and sell" (*Rev. 13:17*) through persecution.

> "Again and again the Lord has instructed that our people are to take their families away from the cities, into the country, where they can raise their own provisions; for in the future the problem of buying and selling will be a very serious one." (*AH, p. 108*)

39. When will there be a "time of great trouble"?

The time of great trouble will start when probation is closed (*Rev. 22:11*) and will occur prior to Jesus' soon return.

"It appeared to them to be taught in the Bible that man's probation would close a short time before the actual coming of the Lord in the clouds of heaven." (*CIHS, p. 102*)

40. When will Jesus return?

The Adventist Church teaches that Jesus will return after the time of great "trouble" (*Jer. 30:7*), to redeem the saved and eventually destroy the lost.

"The promise of Christ's second coming was ever to be kept fresh in the minds of His disciples. The same Jesus whom they had seen ascending into heaven, would come again, to take to Himself those who here below give themselves to His service." (*AA, p. 21*)

41. Where is Jesus now?

Jesus is in the "most holy place" (*Ex. 26:34*) of the Heavenly Sanctuary, judging the lives of those who are living now and have died.

"The realization that Christ had entered the most holy place in the heavenly sanctuary to begin His closing ministry in our behalf, typified in the sanctuary service observed by Israel of old, solemnized the hearts of our pioneer Adventists." (*CIHS, p. x*)

42. Where do Adventists get their doctrines from?

All Adventist doctrines in the 28 Fundamental Beliefs are based on the Bible and these can be found online with their supporting verses from Scripture. Ellen White had visions guiding her to doctrines in the Bible (see quote), never making ones that could not be proved by Scripture.

"When the foundations of the earth were laid, then was also laid the foundation of the Sabbath." (*CET, p. 86*)

43. Where are Adventist churches located?

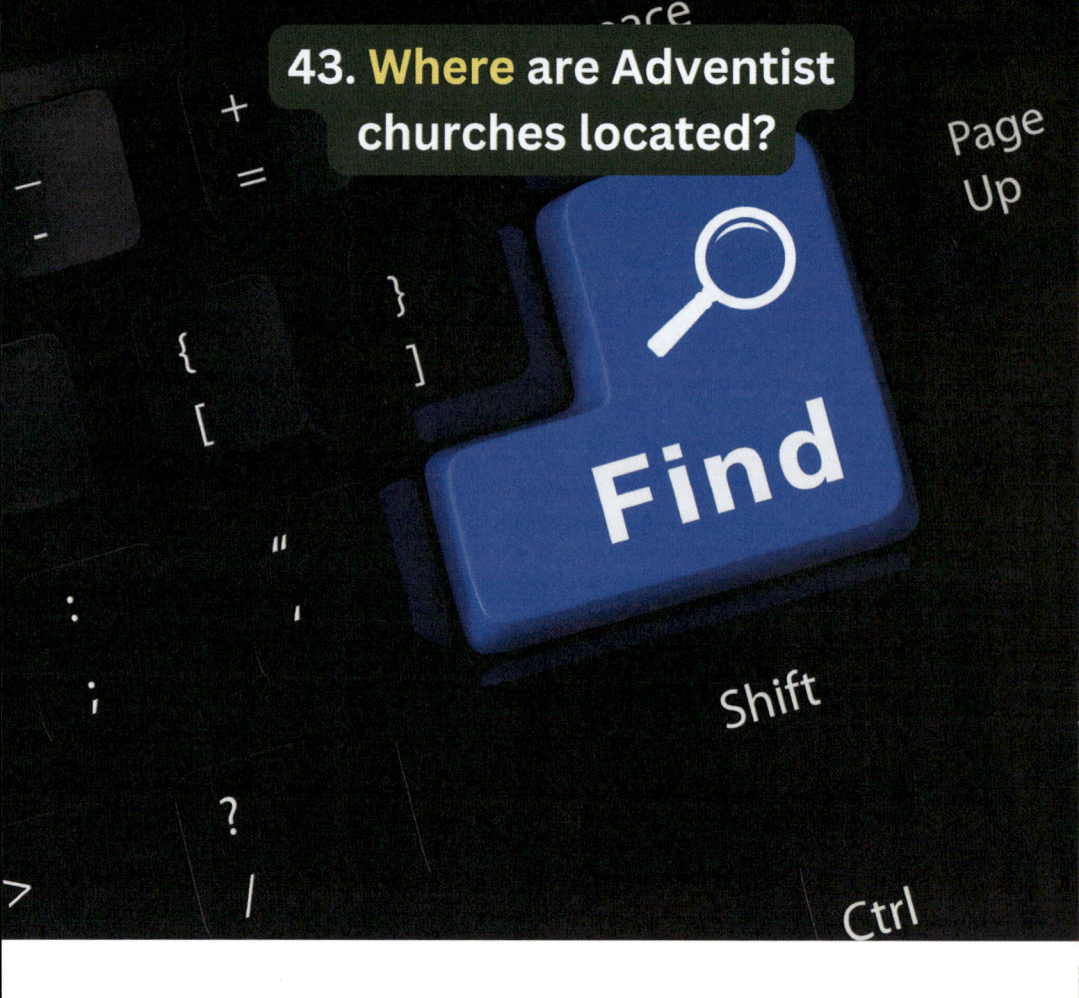

There are over 100,000 churches around the world, with some countries being less represented due to various circumstances. You can search for churches by doing an online search for "find an Adventist Church".

"Thousands have been brought to a knowledge of the truth as it is in Jesus. They have been imbued with the faith that works by love and purifies the soul." (*CET, p. 160*)

44. Where can one read Adventist books?

Ellen White's writings and supporting commentaries can be viewed online for free; a good source is "Ellen White Writings". Her books can be found in various Adventist bookshops around the world and online at Amazon.

"Unvarnished truth must be spoken, in leaflets and pamphlets, and these must be scattered like the leaves of autumn." (*9T, p. 199*)

45. Where are Adventist schools and universities?

Adventist schools and universities are located in many countries around the world. There are currently about 10,000 educational institutions in over 100 countries.

"Teach them that life's true aim is not to secure the greatest possible gain for themselves, but to honor their Maker in doing their part of the world's work, and lending a helpful hand to those weaker or more ignorant." (*Ed, p. 171*)

46. Where is the Adventist headquarters?

The Adventist Church headquarters have been located in Silver Spring, Maryland since 1989. The building is known as the "General Conference", a great improvement from before (see quote).

> "We had much care. The office hands boarded with us, and our family numbered from fifteen to twenty. The large conferences and the Sabbath meetings were held at our house. We had no quiet Sabbaths; for some of the sisters usually tarried all day with their children." (CET, p. 109)

47. Where is the Adventist Church growing fastest?

The Adventist Church currently has the most members in Brazil and is also growing steadily in various other countries globally.

"The Lord wants living members in His church, men and women who will encourage one another in faithful service." (*DG, p. 97*)

48. Where does ADRA (humanitarian agency) operate?

The Adventist Development and Relief Agency (ADRA), currently assists people in over 120 countries.

"Unselfish love, manifested in acts of disinterested kindness, will make it easier for these suffering ones to believe in the love of Christ." (*MTC, p. 109*)

49. Where do people go when they die?

When people die, they "are asleep" (*1 Thess. 4:13*) in the grave, awaiting Jesus' return to the earth, rather than going to heaven or destruction immediately.

"As Paul's epistle was opened and read, great joy and consolation was brought to the church by the words revealing the true state of the dead. Paul showed that those living when Christ should come would not go to meet their Lord in advance of those who had fallen asleep in Jesus." (*AA, p. 176*)

50. Where is the New Jerusalem?

The New Jerusalem is viewed in the Bible as "coming down" (*Rev. 21:2*) to earth, when Jesus returns at the end of the Millennium.

"As the New Jerusalem, in its dazzling splendor, comes down out of heaven, it rests upon the place purified and made ready to receive it, and Christ, with His people and the angels, enters the Holy City." (*DD, p. 53*)

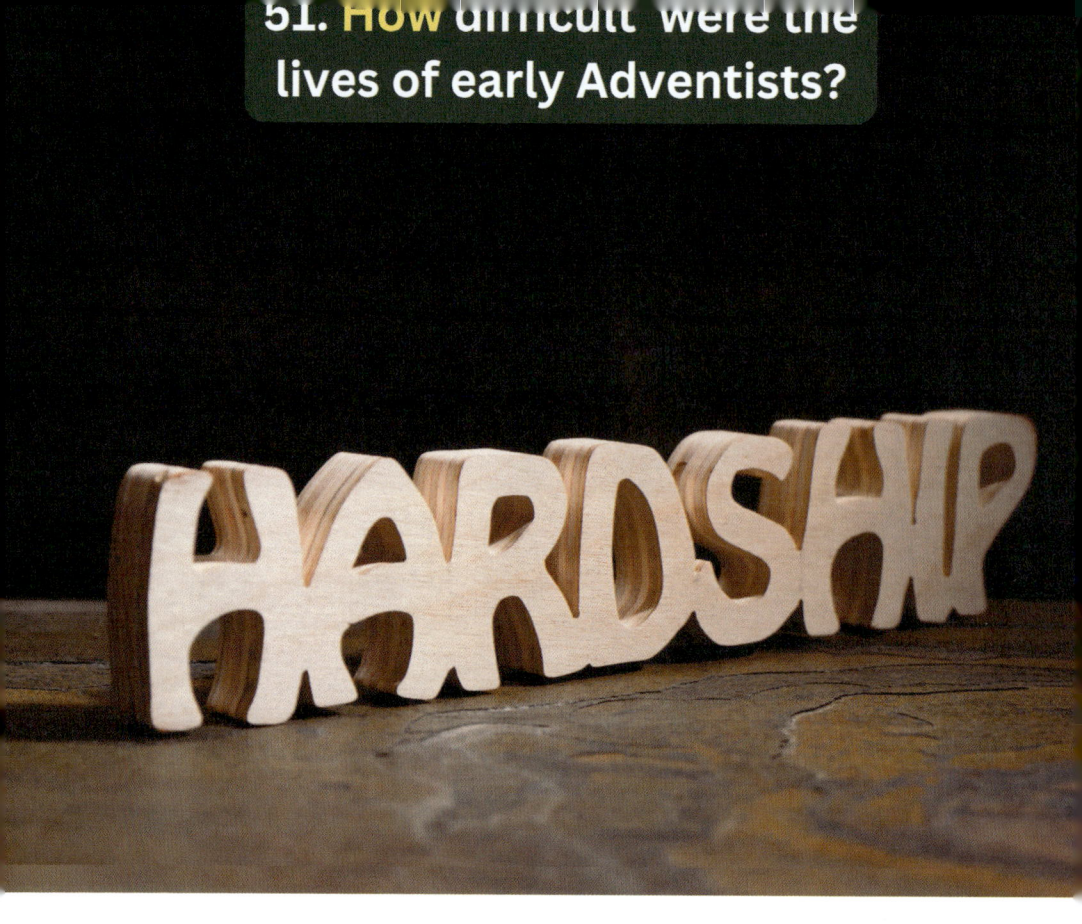

51. How difficult were the lives of early Adventists?

The early pioneers of the Adventist Church suffered much hardship and poverty. Yet, through their faithful and determined efforts the church grew and is now thriving in the twenty-first century.

"For years the pioneers of our work struggled against poverty and manifold hardships, in order to place the cause of present truth on vantage ground. With meager facilities, they labored untiringly; and the Lord blessed their humble efforts." (*LS, p. 337*)

52. How often did Ellen White speak publicly?

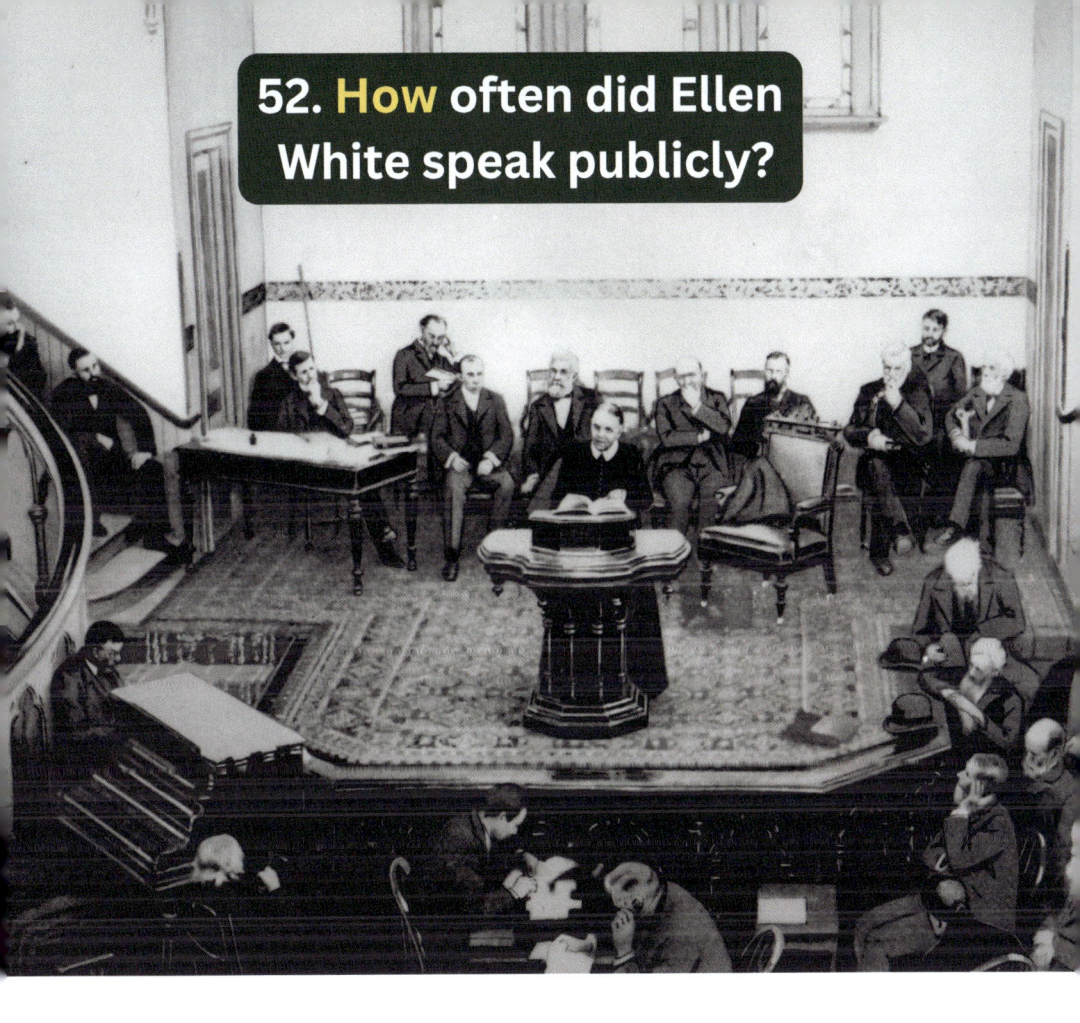

As well as being a prolific writer, Ellen White spoke extensively around the United States and also overseas.

"Preaching is a small part of the work to be done for the salvation of souls. God's Spirit convicts sinners of the truth, and He places them in the arms of the church. The ministers may do their part, but they can never perform the work that the church should do." (4T, p. 65)

53. How many books has Ellen White written?

Ellen White's original writings and subsequent compilations comprise of over 130 titles, totalling over 25 million words.

> "That night I was up at one o'clock, writing as fast as my hand could pass over the paper. For the next few days I worked early and late, preparing for our people the instruction given me regarding the errors that were coming in among us." (*1SM, p. 190*)

54. How is Ellen White criticised?

During her life and afterwards, Ellen White has been extensively criticised. However, despite accusations of plagiarism for instance, she never went to court as it was not proven that she had broken any laws during her lifetime.

"The enemy has made his masterly efforts to unsettle the faith of our own people in the Testimonies, and when these errors come in they claim to prove all the positions by the Bible, but they misinterpret the Scriptures." (3SM, p. 75)

55. How can I become an Adventist?

Anyone can attend an Adventist Church, whether or not you are an Adventist member. To become a member, a pastor will guide you through the church doctrines, after which you will be voted in as one.

"The Lord, by close and pointed truths for these last days, is cleaving out a people from the world and purifying them unto Himself." (*3T, p. 51*)

56. How are Adventists saved?

Adventists believe that we are saved "by grace", "through faith" (*Eph. 2:8*) in Jesus, by repentance and turning away from sin. We should then let Jesus sanctify us, which is the work of a lifetime.

"Children are the heritage of the Lord, and the plan of redemption includes their salvation as well as ours. They have been entrusted to parents in order that they might be brought up in the nurture and admonition of the Lord, that they might be qualified to do their work in time and eternity." (*AH, p. 218*)

57. How fast is the Adventist Church growing?

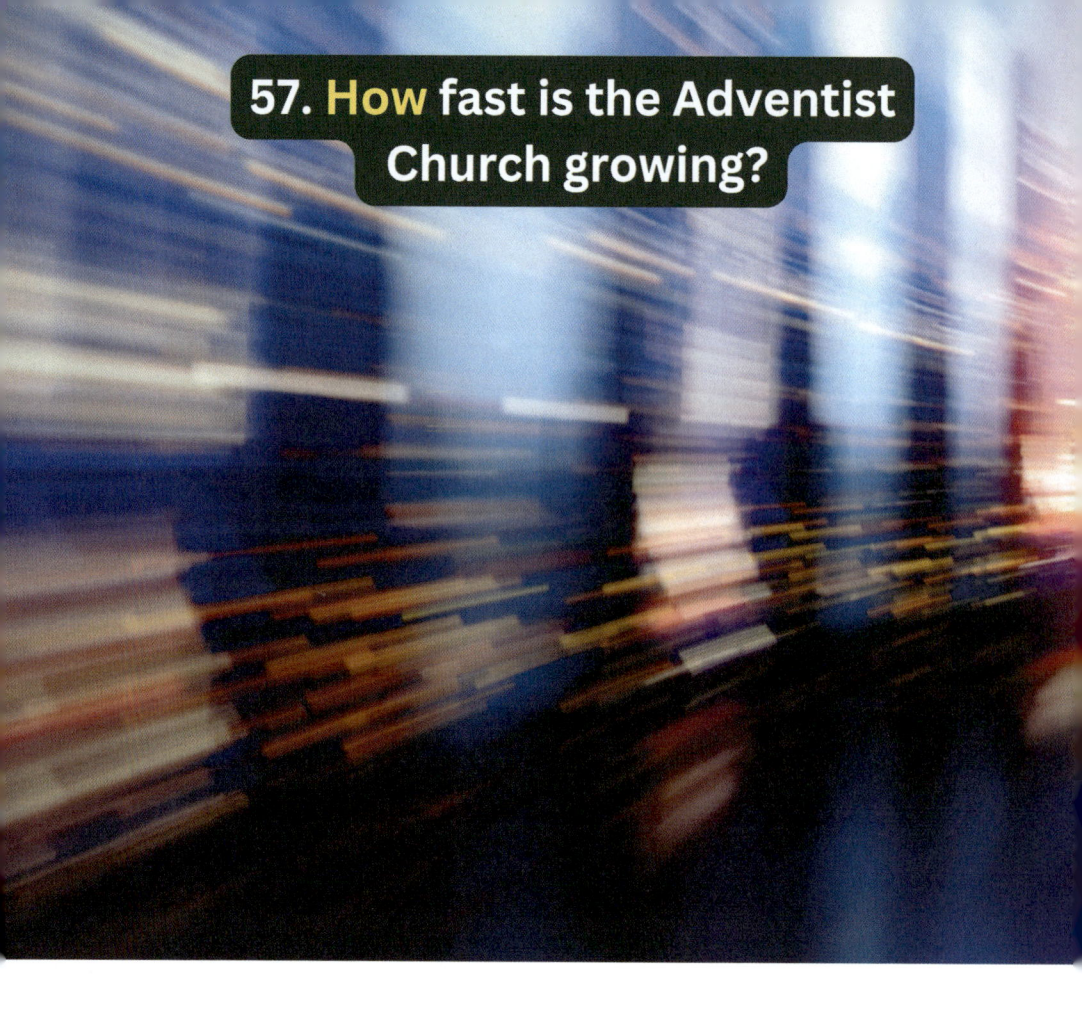

The Seventh-day Adventist Church is growing rapidly, with approximately 1 million new members per year and a total membership of over 22 million.

> "It is the privilege of every Christian, not only to look for, but to hasten the coming of our Lord Jesus Christ. Were all who profess His name bearing fruit to His glory, how quickly the whole world would be sown with the seed of the gospel." (*3T, p. 49*)

58. How will the world end?

After the time of great trouble, Jesus will return and take the living and resurrected saved to Heaven for a 1,000 years. Once Jesus returns again, the devil, his angels and the resurrected lost will attack the New Jerusalem and finally be annihilated. The saved will live gloriously for eternity on the "new earth" (*Rev. 21:1*).

"We are homeward bound. He who loved us so much as to die for us, hath builded for us a city. The New Jerusalem is our place of rest." (*CET, 169*)

59. How will things be on the New Earth?

On the new earth there will be no sin and "no more death" (*Rev. 21:4*). We will have communion with God and be active, interested and harmonious.

"Those who, regardless of all else, place themselves in God's hands, to be and do all that He would have them, will see the King in His beauty. They will behold His matchless charms, and, touching their golden harps, they will fill all heaven with rich music and with songs to the Lamb." (*Ev, p. 454*)

60. How often should we read Ellen White's writings?

God inspired Ellen White in her prophetic ministry for a reason. Therefore, we should try to read as many of Ellen White's key books as possible – read her writings and observe their beneficial effect.

"God is either teaching His church, reproving their wrongs and strengthening their faith, or He is not. This work is of God, or it is not." (*4T, p. 216*)

Acknowledgements

- Copy editing and proofreading by Cordelia Ann Bryan of ProofMePerfect. www.proofmeperfect.com

- Photo of Ascension Rock. https://commons.wikimedia.org/wiki/File:Ascension_Rock.jpg

- Photo of General Conference. https://commons.wikimedia.org/wiki/File:General_Conference.jpg

- Photo of Pastor Ted Wilson. www.en.wikipedia.org/wiki/Ted_N._C._Wilson#/media/File:Ted_N.C._Wilson.jpg

Contact the Author

- Email: info@philipderivaz.co.uk

- Facebook Group:
  www.facebook.com/groups/60questionsansweredin60minutes

- Facebook Page:
  www.facebook.com/60QuestionsAnsweredin60Minutes

- LinkedIn Profile:
  www.linkedin.com/in/philipchristianuk

- Website: www.philipderivaz.co.uk

Appendix

1. Ascension Rock

2. 1843 Prophetic Chart

3. 1833 Leonid Meteor Shower

1. Ascension Rock, where William Miller and others waited for Jesus to return on 22nd October, 1844.

"We were perplexed and disappointed, yet did not renounce our faith. Many still clung to the hope that Jesus would not long delay His coming; the word of the Lord was sure, it could not fail." (*LS, p.* 45)

2. The 1843 prophetic chart showing Jesus' return.

"In the scattering, Israel was smitten and torn, but now in the gathering time God will heal and bind up His people." (*EW, p. 89*)

3. The great Leonid meteor shower of November 12th, 1833.

'Thus was displayed the last of those signs of His coming, concerning which Jesus bade His disciples, "When ye shall see all these things, know that it is near, even at the doors."' (*Mar, p. 307*)

"We have nothing to fear for the future, except as we shall forget the way the Lord has led us, and His teaching in our past history."
(LS, p. 161)